MW00944209

YOUR AWKWARD
LIFE
GETS
BETTER

a guided journal to
your better life in
60 days

ANDY VARGO

Your Awkward Life Gets Better

Text copyright © 2018 by Andy Vargo

All Rights Reserved

ISBN 9781724142122

Awkward Career Publications

awkwardcareer.com

Introduction

Life gets better, but it doesn't just happen automatically. We have to put some work into it. Not what you wanted to hear? I know exactly what you mean. We always want that quick fix, that winning lottery ticket, the magic pill. But that is just not reality. The truth is we have to create the life we want. The truth is, it takes work to get to that life. The good news is that we have the power to do just that!

But what about those days when we cannot muster the strength to push the weight of the covers away to rise out of bed in the morning? What about those days when we do not even have enough courage to face simple daily tasks like getting dressed and brushing our teeth?

These are the days when we are at our lowest. That's what we call rock bottom, when things just cannot possibly get any worse. But the great thing about rock bottom is it that you still have power. You have the power to stop the descent. You have power the power to start taking control of your life one step at a time. I know because I had to do that exact same thing not all that long ago.

Where do you start when everything in life seems so very overwhelming?

Right here.

You start right here.

By having this journal in your hands you have already taken that first step. You have decided that your life is not exactly the way you want it to be. Even better, you have decided to do something about it!

How To Use This Journal

So you are not happy with life? What are you going to do about it? Each day will be the same as the last if you do nothing to make it better!

Going forward you are in control of your own fate. You control your destiny. You have the power to change how tomorrow will be!

It is very simple:

A great day starts the night before. To set yourself up for a better day, we are going to start before you go to bed.

Each day you will reflect on what you did that day to make the day better. Some days this may be very simple things. For example: I got up on time, I brushed my teeth, or I went outside. Try anything, no matter how simple.

Next, you will plan for tomorrow. This is a critical step, as you need to wake up knowing how you will take control of your life that day. This will leave no question what steps you will take to move your life in a more positive direction.

Each day I have written an idea to help generate some thought. Do whatever you want and do not be afraid to repeat ideas as often as you need.

Now go have fun creating the life you want!

Day One

Date: Current Mood:

Today I did these three things to make life better:

One: **Started the Life Gets Better Journal**

Two:

Three:

Tomorrow I will do these three things to make life better:

One:

Two:

Three:

Idea: Spend fifteen minutes alone in nature listening to the sounds of the world around you.

Some things to remember from today:

Something learned:

Something enjoyed:

Something never to forget:

Today's Word: **HOPE**

Day Two

Date: **Current Mood:**

Today I did these three things to make life better:

One:

Two:

Three:

Tomorrow I will do these three things to make life better:

One:

Two:

Three:

Idea: Enjoy a cup of coffee or tea in a place you have never been.

Some things to remember from today:

Something learned:

Something enjoyed:

Something never to forget:

Today's Word: **ACTION**

Day Three

Date: **Current Mood:**

Today I did these three things to make life better:

One:

Two:

Three:

Tomorrow I will do these three things to make life better:

One:

Two:

Three:

Idea: Call a friend that you have lost touch with.

Some things to remember from today:

Something learned:

Something enjoyed:

Something never to forget:

Today's Word: **PEACE**

Day Four

Date: **Current Mood:**

Today I did these three things to make life better:

One:

Two:

Three:

Tomorrow I will do these three things to make life better:

One:

Two:

Three:

Idea: Wake up and get out of bed a half an hour earlier than usual.

Some things to remember from today:

Something learned:

Something enjoyed:

Something never to forget:

Today's Word: **COURAGE**

Day Five

Date: Current Mood:

Today I did these three things to make life better:

One:

Two:

Three:

Tomorrow I will do these three things to make life better:

One:

Two:

Three:

Idea: Make a home cooked meal for dinner complete with dessert.

Some things to remember from today:

Something learned:

Something enjoyed:

Something never to forget:

Today's Word: **TRUTH**

Day Six

Date: **Current Mood:**

Today I did these three things to make life better:

One:

Two:

Three:

Tomorrow I will do these three things to make life better:

One:

Two:

Three:

Idea: Listen to uplifting music while you shower and get ready for the day.

Some things to remember from today:

Something learned:

Something enjoyed:

Something never to forget:

Today's Word: LOVE

Day Seven

Date: Current Mood:

Today I did these three things to make life better:

One:

Two:

Three:

Tomorrow I will do these three things to make life better:

One:

Two:

Three:

Idea: Take time to watch the sunset wherever you are.

Some things to remember from today:

Something learned:

Something enjoyed:

Something never to forget:

Today's Word: **EFFORT**

Day Eight

Date: Current Mood:

Today I did these three things to make life better:

One:

Two:

Three:

Tomorrow I will do these three things to make life better:

One:

Two:

Three:

Idea: Make someone laugh with a joke, a prank or simply by sharing an old memory.

Some things to remember from today:

Something learned:

Something enjoyed:

Something never to forget:

Today's Word: **MOMENTUM**

Day Nine

Date: **Current Mood:**

Today I did these three things to make life better:

One:

Two:

Three:

Tomorrow I will do these three things to make life better:

One:

Two:

Three:

Idea: Stop to smell the roses, literally. Find a park, garden or flower shop where you can take it in.

Some things to remember from today:

Something learned:

Something enjoyed:

Something never to forget:

Today's Word: **LAUGHTER**

Day Ten

Date: Current Mood:

Today I did these three things to make life better:

One:

Two:

Three:

Tomorrow I will do these three things to make life better:

One:

Two:

Three:

Idea: Leave the house for no reason and go for a drive to clear your head.

Some things to remember from today:

Something learned:

Something enjoyed:

Something never to forget:

Today's Word: **SHARING**

Day Eleven

Date: **Current Mood:**

Today I did these three things to make life better:

One:

Two:

Three:

Tomorrow I will do these three things to make life better:

One:

Two:

Three:

Idea: Call your mom (or mother figure) just to say hi. If she is not with us, write down what you would say to her if she was.

Some things to remember from today:

Something learned:

Something enjoyed:

Something never to forget:

Today's Word: **LIFE**

Day Twelve

Date: Current Mood:

Today I did these three things to make life better:

One:

Two:

Three:

Tomorrow I will do these three things to make life better:

One:

Two:

Three:

Idea: Meet a friend to share a cup of coffee or tea at your favorite local shop.

Some things to remember from today:

Something learned:

Something enjoyed:

Something never to forget:

Today's Word: **SILENCE**

Day Thirteen

Date: **Current Mood:**

Today I did these three things to make life better:

One:

Two:

Three:

Tomorrow I will do these three things to make life better:

One:

Two:

Three:

Idea: Play a game. With or without a friend, whether it is checkers, tic-tac-toe, or solitaire, just set aside some time to do something silly for fun.

Some things to remember from today:

Something learned:

Something enjoyed:

Something never to forget:

Today's Word: **GROWTH**

Day Fourteen

Date: **Current Mood:**

Today I did these three things to make life better:

One:

Two:

Three:

Tomorrow I will do these three things to make life better:

One:

Two:

Three:

Idea: Dine in a restaurant you have never been to before, especially if it is one you drive by every day!

Some things to remember from today:

Something learned:

Something enjoyed:

Something never to forget:

Today's Word: **RELAX**

Day Fifteen

Date: **Current Mood:**

Today I did these three things to make life better:

One:

Two:

Three:

Tomorrow I will do these three things to make life better:

One:

Two:

Three:

Idea: Sing along to the radio on every drive you take all day long.

Some things to remember from today:

Something learned:

Something enjoyed:

Something never to forget:

Today's Word: **FRIENDSHIP**

Day Sixteen

Date: Current Mood:

Today I did these three things to make life better:

One:

Two:

Three:

Tomorrow I will do these three things to make life better:

One:

Two:

Three:

Idea: Have a productive day at work. Set a goal, write a list, and stay on it. Keep focused all day!

Some things to remember from today:

Something learned:

Something enjoyed:

Something never to forget:

Today's Word: **PROGRESS**

Day Seventeen

Date: Current Mood:

Today I did these three things to make life better:

One:

Two:

Three:

Tomorrow I will do these three things to make life better:

One:

Two:

Three:

Idea: Read alone for one hour.

Some things to remember from today:

Something learned:

Something enjoyed:

Something never to forget:

Today's Word: **GROWTH**

Day Eighteen

Date: Current Mood:

Today I did these three things to make life better:

One:

Two:

Three:

Tomorrow I will do these three things to make life better:

One:

Two:

Three:

Idea: Wake up before the sunrises and take time to enjoy watching it crest over the horizon.

Some things to remember from today:

Something learned:

Something enjoyed:

Something never to forget:

Today's Word: **FAITH**

Day Nineteen

Date: Current Mood:

Today I did these three things to make life better:

One:

Two:

Three:

Tomorrow I will do these three things to make life better:

One:

Two:

Three:

Idea: Make your bed. It's that simple!

Some things to remember from today:

Something learned:

Something enjoyed:

Something never to forget:

Today's Word: **WISDOM**

Day Twenty

Date: **Current Mood:**

Today I did these three things to make life better:

One:

Two:

Three:

Tomorrow I will do these three things to make life better:

One:

Two:

Three:

Idea: Call your dad (or father figure) just to say hi. If he is not with us, write down what you would say to him if he was.

Some things to remember from today:

Something learned:

Something enjoyed:

Something never to forget:

Today's Word: **HUMOR**

Day Twenty One

Date: **Current Mood:**

Today I did these three things to make life better:

One:

Two:

Three:

Tomorrow I will do these three things to make life better:

One:

Two:

Three:

Idea: Write a poem. Long or short, good or bad, rhyming or not, write it down.

Some things to remember from today:

Something learned:

Something enjoyed:

Something never to forget:

Today's Word: **FAMILY**

Day Twenty Two

Date: **Current Mood:**

Today I did these three things to make life better:

One:

Two:

Three:

Tomorrow I will do these three things to make life better:

One:

Two:

Three:

Idea: Clean up your workspace at home or work. Get that clutter out of the way so you can think straight without tripping over the junk.

Some things to remember from today:

Something learned:

Something enjoyed:

Something never to forget:

Today's Word: CHARITY

Day Twenty Three

Date: Current Mood:

Today I did these three things to make life better:

One:

Two:

Three:

Tomorrow I will do these three things to make life better:

One:

Two:

Three:

Idea: Eat healthy all day. No cheating. No stress eating No junk food!

Some things to remember from today:

Something learned:

Something enjoyed:

Something never to forget:

Today's Word: **MEDITATION**

Day Twenty Four

Date: Current Mood:

Today I did these three things to make life better:

One:

Two:

Three:

Tomorrow I will do these three things to make life better:

One:

Two:

Three:

Idea: Go sing karaoke with a friend. Be sure to at least sing one solo and one duet.

Some things to remember from today:

Something learned:

Something enjoyed:

Something never to forget:

Today's Word: **INSIGHT**

Day Twenty Five

Date: Current Mood:

Today I did these three things to make life better:

One:

Two:

Three:

Tomorrow I will do these three things to make life better:

One:

Two:

Three:

Idea: Enjoy a live performance: music, comedy or a play.

Some things to remember from today:

Something learned:

Something enjoyed:

Something never to forget:

Today's Word: **NATURE**

Day Twenty Six

Date: Current Mood:

Today I did these three things to make life better:

One:

Two:

Three:

Tomorrow I will do these three things to make life better:

One:

Two:

Three:

Idea: Exercise for a half an hour. Walk, run, bike, or lift. Whatever you can do to push yourself a bit more than usual.

Some things to remember from today:

Something learned:

Something enjoyed:

Something never to forget:

Today's Word: **GOODNESS**

Day Twenty Seven

Date: **Current Mood:**

Today I did these three things to make life better:

One:

Two:

Three:

Tomorrow I will do these three things to make life better:

One:

Two:

Three:

Idea: Try a new craft for the first time. Watch a tutorial online if you must or sign up for a class at the local community center.

Some things to remember from today:

Something learned:

Something enjoyed:

Something never to forget:

Today's Word: **HEALTH**

Day Twenty Eight

Date: Current Mood:

Today I did these three things to make life better:

One:

Two:

Three:

Tomorrow I will do these three things to make life better:

One:

Two:

Three:

Idea: Buy someone flowers, anyone, even a stranger.

Some things to remember from today:

Something learned:

Something enjoyed:

Something never to forget:

Today's Word: **THRIVE**

Day Twenty Nine

Date: Current Mood:

Today I did these three things to make life better:

One:

Two:

Three:

Tomorrow I will do these three things to make life better:

One:

Two:

Three:

Idea: Draw a picture no matter how skilled you are. Spend at least thirty minutes filling in the details.

Some things to remember from today:

Something learned:

Something enjoyed:

Something never to forget:

Today's Word: **MUSIC**

Day Thirty

Date: Current Mood:

Today I did these three things to make life better:

One:

Two:

Three:

Tomorrow I will do these three things to make life better:

One:

Two:

Three:

Idea: Call your sister (whoever you feel is one) just to say hi. If she is not with us, write down what you would say to her if she was.

Some things to remember from today:

Something learned:

Something enjoyed:

Something never to forget:

Today's Word: **STRENGTH**

Day Thirty One

Date: Current Mood:

Today I did these three things to make life better:

One:

Two:

Three:

Tomorrow I will do these three things to make life better:

One:

Two:

Three:

Idea: Me-time! Pamper yourself with a treat: shopping spree, spa, or a cheat day with an extra dessert! You deserve it!

Some things to remember from today:

Something learned:

Something enjoyed:

Something never to forget:

Today's Word: **DANCE**

Day Thirty Two

Date: **Current Mood:**

Today I did these three things to make life better:

One:

Two:

Three:

Tomorrow I will do these three things to make life better:

One:

Two:

Three:

Idea: Arrive ten minutes early to your appointments all day. And yes this includes going to work a little early too!

Some things to remember from today:

Something learned:

Something enjoyed:

Something never to forget:

Today's Word: **CHARACTER**

Day Thirty Three

Date: Current Mood:

Today I did these three things to make life better:

One:

Two:

Three:

Tomorrow I will do these three things to make life better:

One:

Two:

Three:

Idea: Honor the memory of someone who is no longer with us. A few moments of silence, a shared memory with friends or a visit to their memorial.

Some things to remember from today:

Something learned:

Something enjoyed:

Something never to forget:

Today's Word: **GRACE**

Day Thirty Four

Date: **Current Mood:**

Today I did these three things to make life better:

One:

Two:

Three:

Tomorrow I will do these three things to make life better:

One:

Two:

Three:

Idea: A day without politics or news, try it!

Some things to remember from today:

Something learned:

Something enjoyed:

Something never to forget:

Today's Word: SMILE

Day Thirty Five

Date: Current Mood:

Today I did these three things to make life better:

One:

Two:

Three:

Tomorrow I will do these three things to make life better:

One:

Two:

Three:

Idea: Check out the local museum.

Some things to remember from today:

Something learned:

Something enjoyed:

Something never to forget:

Today's Word: **NOURISH**

Day Thirty Six

Date: **Current Mood:**

Today I did these three things to make life better:

One:

Two:

Three:

Tomorrow I will do these three things to make life better:

One:

Two:

Three:

Idea: Surprise a friend with a visit. Stop by their home, work, or get them to meet you at a park for a stroll.

Some things to remember from today:

Something learned:

Something enjoyed:

Something never to forget:

Today's Word: **WORTHY**

Day Thirty Seven

Date: Current Mood:

Today I did these three things to make life better:

One:

Two:

Three:

Tomorrow I will do these three things to make life better:

One:

Two:

Three:

Idea: Take a walk on your lunch break!

Some things to remember from today:

Something learned:

Something enjoyed:

Something never to forget:

Today's Word: **TRUST**

Day Thirty Eight

Date: Current Mood:

Today I did these three things to make life better:

One:

Two:

Three:

Tomorrow I will do these three things to make life better:

One:

Two:

Three:

Idea: Journal about anything for an hour.

Some things to remember from today:

Something learned:

Something enjoyed:

Something never to forget:

Today's Word: **PROSPER**

Day Thirty Nine

Date: Current Mood:

Today I did these three things to make life better:

One:

Two:

Three:

Tomorrow I will do these three things to make life better:

One:

Two:

Three:

Idea: Play a musical instrument: piano, guitar, trumpet, or harmonica. Even if you just pick sticks to drum on whatever is close by.

Some things to remember from today:

Something learned:

Something enjoyed:

Something never to forget:

Today's Word: **CONFIDENCE**

Day Forty

Date: **Current Mood:**

Today I did these three things to make life better:

One:

Two:

Three:

Tomorrow I will do these three things to make life better:

One:

Two:

Three:

Idea: Call your brother (whoever you feel is one) just to say hi. If he is not with us, write down what you would say to him if he was.

Some things to remember from today:

Something learned:

Something enjoyed:

Something never to forget:

Today's Word: **TRANQUILITY**

Day Forty One

Date: Current Mood:

Today I did these three things to make life better:

One:

Two:

Three:

Tomorrow I will do these three things to make life better:

One:

Two:

Three:

Idea: Spend three hours alone reflecting on your dreams and how to make them a reality.

Some things to remember from today:

Something learned:

Something enjoyed:

Something never to forget:

Today's Word: **INSPIRE**

Day Forty Two

Date: Current Mood:

Today I did these three things to make life better:

One:

Two:

Three:

Tomorrow I will do these three things to make life better:

One:

Two:

Three:

Idea: Greet three strangers throughout the day.

Some things to remember from today:

Something learned:

Something enjoyed:

Something never to forget:

Today's Word: **ENGAGE**

Day Forty Three

Date: Current Mood:

Today I did these three things to make life better:

One:

Two:

Three:

Tomorrow I will do these three things to make life better:

One:

Two:

Three:

Idea: Go to bed on time. Wind things down ahead of time so that you are relaxed and your mind can calm down.

Some things to remember from today:

Something learned:

Something enjoyed:

Something never to forget:

Today's Word: EVOLVE

Day Forty Four

Date: Current Mood:

Today I did these three things to make life better:

One:

Two:

Three:

Tomorrow I will do these three things to make life better:

One:

Two:

Three:

Idea: Complete a random act of kindness. Buy coffee. Carry groceries. Help with a project. Anything!

Some things to remember from today:

Something learned:

Something enjoyed:

Something never to forget:

Today's Word: **COMFORT**

Day Forty Five

Date: Current Mood:

Today I did these three things to make life better:

One:

Two:

Three:

Tomorrow I will do these three things to make life better:

One:

Two:

Three:

Idea: Stay offline for two hours. This means turning off your phone and walking away.

Some things to remember from today:

Something learned:

Something enjoyed:

Something never to forget:

Today's Word: **CHEER**

Day Forty Six

Date: **Current Mood:**

Today I did these three things to make life better:

One:

Two:

Three:

Tomorrow I will do these three things to make life better:

One:

Two:

Three:

Idea: Walk or jog further than you ever have before. It does not matter if it is two miles, two blocks or two steps, go further than ever in your life.

Some things to remember from today:

Something learned:

Something enjoyed:

Something never to forget:

Today's Word: **BALANCE**

Day Forty Seven

Date: **Current Mood:**

Today I did these three things to make life better:

One:

Two:

Three:

Tomorrow I will do these three things to make life better:

One:

Two:

Three:

Idea: Clean house: Get all the chores done so you have a clean place to relax and focus for a productive week ahead! No skipping out on making that bed either.

Some things to remember from today:

Something learned:

Something enjoyed:

Something never to forget:

Today's Word: **EXPERIENCE**

Day Forty Eight

Date: **Current Mood:**

Today I did these three things to make life better:

One:

Two:

Three:

Tomorrow I will do these three things to make life better:

One:

Two:

Three:

Idea: Spend twenty minutes enjoying a hobby.

Some things to remember from today:

Something learned:

Something enjoyed:

Something never to forget:

Today's Word: **CONTENT**

Day Forty Nine

Date: **Current Mood:**

Today I did these three things to make life better:

One:

Two:

Three:

Tomorrow I will do these three things to make life better:

One:

Two:

Three:

Idea: Listen. Don't talk. Just listen to a friend who needs to work through some things right now.

Some things to remember from today:

Something learned:

Something enjoyed:

Something never to forget:

Today's Word: **HARMONY**

Day Fifty

Date: Current Mood:

Today I did these three things to make life better:

One:

Two:

Three:

Tomorrow I will do these three things to make life better:

One:

Two:

Three:

Idea: Leave work on time. Start wrapping up a half an hour early just to make sure you get out the door on time!

Some things to remember from today:

Something learned:

Something enjoyed:

Something never to forget:

Today's Word: **SPONTANEOUS**

Day Fifty One

Date: **Current Mood:**

Today I did these three things to make life better:

One:

Two:

Three:

Tomorrow I will do these three things to make life better:

One:

Two:

Three:

Idea: Pick an unfished project and get it done!

Some things to remember from today:

Something learned:

Something enjoyed:

Something never to forget:

Today's Word: **VENTURE**

Day Fifty Two

Date: Current Mood:

Today I did these three things to make life better:

One:

Two:

Three:

Tomorrow I will do these three things to make life better:

One:

Two:

Three:

Idea: Smile. Make it through your day with a smile on!

Some things to remember from today:

Something learned:

Something enjoyed:

Something never to forget:

Today's Word: JOKE

Day Fifty Three

Date: **Current Mood:**

Today I did these three things to make life better:

One:

Two:

Three:

Tomorrow I will do these three things to make life better:

One:

Two:

Three:

Idea: Balance your budget. It will feel better knowing what you have even if you only have a few dollars to work with.

Some things to remember from today:

Something learned:

Something enjoyed:

Something never to forget:

Today's Word: **CHALLENGE**

Day Fifty Four

Date: **Current Mood:**

Today I did these three things to make life better:

One:

Two:

Three:

Tomorrow I will do these three things to make life better:

One:

Two:

Three:

Idea: Thank five people for what they mean to you. It can be as simple as their smile or as deep as you want to get.

Some things to remember from today:

Something learned:

Something enjoyed:

Something never to forget:

Today's Word: **BEAUTY**

Day Fifty Five

Date: **Current Mood:**

Today I did these three things to make life better:

One:

Two:

Three:

Tomorrow I will do these three things to make life better:

One:

Two:

Three:

Idea: Spend some time with a pet. If you do not have one then head over to the dog park and make a new friend.

Some things to remember from today:

Something learned:

Something enjoyed:

Something never to forget:

Today's Word: **LEARN**

Day Fifty Six

Date: Current Mood:

Today I did these three things to make life better:

One:

Two:

Three:

Tomorrow I will do these three things to make life better:

One:

Two:

Three:

Idea: Hit up the local farmers market.

Some things to remember from today:

Something learned:

Something enjoyed:

Something never to forget:

Today's Word: **CONNECTION**

Day Fifty Seven

Date: **Current Mood:**

Today I did these three things to make life better:

One:

Two:

Three:

Tomorrow I will do these three things to make life better:

One:

Two:

Three:

Idea: Learn something new. Watch a video, join a friend or read a book.

Some things to remember from today:

Something learned:

Something enjoyed:

Something never to forget:

Today's Word: **REFLECT**

Day Fifty Eight

Date: Current Mood:

Today I did these three things to make life better:

One:

Two:

Three:

Tomorrow I will do these three things to make life better:

One:

Two:

Three:

Idea: No social media for an entire day!

Some things to remember from today:

Something learned:

Something enjoyed:

Something never to forget:

Today's Word: **SUCCESS**

Day Fifty Nine

Date: **Current Mood:**

Today I did these three things to make life better:

One:

Two:

Three:

Tomorrow I will do these three things to make life better:

One:

Two:

Three:

Idea: Lend a hand to a friend or family member who could use it. Help them move, do their chores, or make them a meal.

Some things to remember from today:

Something learned:

Something enjoyed:

Something never to forget:

Today's Word: ACHIEVE

Day Sixty

Date: **Current Mood:**

Today I did these three things to make life better:

One:

Two:

Three:

Tomorrow I will do these three things to make life better:

One:

Two:

Three:

Idea: Celebrate! Go out with friends for dessert and drinks or have a quiet night alone. Whatever you do, mark the occasion in a way that is special to you.

Some things to remember from today:

Something learned:

Something enjoyed:

Something never to forget:

Today's Word: **ONWARD**

Conclusion

You did it! You made it through two months of making your life better, step by step, one day at a time. How do you feel?

My hope is that you feel stronger, better, and happier. I hope that you have tried new things and connected in more meaningful ways with the people in your life. I hope that you feel that you have the power to create the life you want to live.

What's next?

It's simple, keep going. Keep trying new things every day. Keep finding ways to connect with those in your life. Continue to use the power you have to create your best life.

If you need to, start a new journal filled with more adventures. Look back through these pages and highlight your favorite moments. Find the things that made the biggest impact on you, and recreate those moments.

Share.

Share with your friends. Share with your family. Share with those who may need some help with the weight of the covers to get out of bed and start their day. Show them the power they already have to create the life they want to live.

After all, this is not the end. This is just...

The Start

About the Author

Do you feel like you are always two steps away from your big break? Then you can understand how Andy Vargo lived the first forty years of his life. Coming out of the closet at forty doesn't define him, pursuing his passion to help others does. Andy works corporate and school events as a motivational speaker and helps people live their fullest lives as a one on one life coach. At night you can find him working stages around the northwest as a comedian making light of his journey with the gift of laughter. Awkward is not only his brand, but his style as Andy encourages us all to 'Own Our Awkward' and be true to our genuine selves.

Andy hosts the podcast, *Own Your Awkward*, and shares thoughts and ideas in his blog and video series available at awkwardcareer.com.

Continue Your Journey

Is your life boring?

Order the second book in the *Awkward Journal* series,
Your Awkward Life Gets Funner.

Now Available

Work got you down?

Order the third book in the *Awkward Journal* series,
Your Awkward Work Gets Better.

Now Available

Need help accepting yourself?

Order the fourth book in the *Awkward Journal* series,
Your Awkward Life Gets Gayer.

Available November 2018

Made in the USA
Lexington, KY
15 November 2019

57133468R00072